21st
Century
Skills Library

COOL CAREERS

SURGICAL TECHNOLOGIST

MATT MULLINS

Published in the United States of America by
Cherry Lake Publishing, Ann Arbor, Michigan
www.cherrylakepublishing.com

Content Adviser
William D. Hammer, CST, M.Ed., Associate Professor, Surgical Technology Program
Director, Illinois Central College

Credits
Photos: Cover and page 1, ©H. Mark Weidman Photography/Alamy; page 4,
©iStockphoto.com/MiguelMalo; page 6, ©Monkey Business Images/Shutterstock,
Inc.; page 8, ©iStockphoto.com/BeyzaSultanDURNA; page 10, ©iStockphoto.com/
nmaxfield; page 12, ©iStockphoto.com/NiDerLander; page 14, ©iStockphoto.com/
tvorenie; page 16, ©Carolina K. Smith, M.D./Shutterstock, Inc.; page 18, ©Tina
Manley/North America/Alamy; page 20, ©iStockphoto.com/clu; page 23, ©ARCTIC
IMAGES/Alamy; page 24, ©carlo dapino/Shutterstock, Inc.; page 26, ©Alexey
Averiyanov/Shutterstock, Inc.; page 27, ©beerkoff/Shutterstock, Inc.

Library of Congress Cataloging-in-Publication Data
Mullins, Matt.
  Surgical technologist/by Matt Mullins.
    p. cm.—(Cool careers)
  Includes bibliographical references and index.
  ISBN-13: 978-1-60279-939-4 (lib. bdg.)
  ISBN-10: 1-60279-939-3 (lib. bdg.)
  1. Operating room technicians—Juvenile literature. I. Title. II. Series.
  RD32.3.M85 2010
  617'.917—dc22   2010001437

Cherry Lake Publishing would like to acknowledge
the work of The Partnership for 21st Century Skills.
Please visit *www.21stcenturyskills.org* for more information.

Printed in the United States of America
Corporate Graphics Inc.
July 2010
CLFA07

TABLE OF CONTENTS

CHAPTER ONE
A KEY MEMBER OF THE SURGICAL TEAM

Katie's stomach hurt. She was 10, and it had ached all night. At the hospital, the doctor felt Katie's belly

A surgical technologist is just one member of a surgical team.

and raised his eyebrows. He felt a large lump. It was her **appendix**, and it was too big. It had to come out.

They wheeled Katie to **surgery** 2 hours later. She had already met the doctor who would perform the surgery to remove her appendix. When she rolled into the operating room, she saw several more people. She saw nurses. She saw an **anesthesiologist** who would control the medicine that would put her to sleep. She also saw a surgical technologist. All of these people worked together as a surgical team.

People sometimes overlook surgical technologists. They know about nurses, who care for patients. They know about doctors, who talk with patients and examine them to figure out what's wrong. They even know about anesthesiologists, the experts who keep patients from feeling pain during an operation.

Surgical technologists are very important. You've probably seen scenes of surgery on TV. When the surgeon says "scalpel," someone hands him a special knife. That someone is often the surgical technologist.

Surgical technologists do more than just hand over **instruments**. They prepare operating rooms. Surgical technologists make sure everything is clean and **sterile**. They make sure everything is ready for the surgeon. They help doctors and nurses scrub their hands and put on sterile gloves so they can touch the patient during the operation. All this preparation helps keep the patient from getting a

contagious disease or infection. There's more to being a surgical technologist than just cleaning, though.

Surgeries are very complicated. It takes a lot of preparation to make sure everything is ready. If things go wrong, new supplies might be needed. Someone needs to be ready to help in a hurry.

Surgical technologists help make sure doctors can clearly see the part of the body they are operating on.

That someone is the surgical technologist. Surgical technologists do many things. They are the general helpers who make an operation go smoothly.

Some surgical technologists "scrub in" so they are clean enough to help surgeons. They wash up and wear sterile gloves and gowns that cover their clothes. Others get patients and bring them to operating rooms. They help move patients to the operating table. They keep track of supplies during an operation. If a doctor runs out of sponges, the surgical technologist brings more.

A surgical technologist counts needles and sponges and other instruments. This is to make sure nothing gets accidentally left inside the patient! Surgical technologists

Surgical techs keep an eye on the supplies so the surgeon can concentrate on the patient.

check bandages or dressings to make sure they fit right. Then they help clean and prepare the operating room for the next surgical team.

21ST CENTURY CONTENT

Surgical technologists often divide up responsibilities during an operation.

Scrub techs check supplies and equipment. They set up tables and instruments and help prepare patients. They help the other surgical team members put on gowns and gloves and clean up.

Circulating surgical technologists do not scrub in. They rush off to get new equipment if a doctor needs it. They do things that require staying outside the sterile area.

Surgical first assistants do specialized work under the direction of the surgeon. They tie off blood vessels, help the surgeon see what she is operating on, help in emergencies, and more.

Surgical technologists work very hard. They have a lot to do in a day on the job. It's hard to imagine surgery without a surgical technologist.

CHAPTER TWO
A DAY ON THE JOB

A my is a surgical technologist. She works 5 days a week. She may also be called in to work at night

Scrubs are special clothing that many hospital employees wear.

or on weekends. Amy works at a large teaching hospital at a university. People come to this hospital from hundreds of miles away. The doctors and surgeons at this hospital are very skilled. Amy works in a **transplant center**.

A person who needs a new liver, heart, or other organ goes to a transplant center. The new organ comes from a **donor**. A donor is a person who has agreed that his organs can be used by others. The organ to be transplanted is removed from the donor and placed in the body of the person who needs it. Often, a donated organ will save another person's life.

The person who will get the organ goes into an operating room. An anesthesiologist puts him to sleep. The surgeon, nurses, and surgical technologists work together. They remove the patient's diseased organ and put in the new one.

When Amy comes to work each day, she starts by changing her clothes. She goes to a locker room like the one you might have at school. There, Amy changes into loose-fitting hospital clothing called *scrubs*. She puts on a hat to cover her hair. She puts on comfortable shoes that she keeps at the hospital.

When Amy leaves the locker room, she goes to her office, or control station. There, Amy picks up papers about her next **case**. The paper tells her who will be operated on. It tells what the operation will be for, such as a kidney or pancreas transplant. It lists all the supplies and instruments the surgery will require. It gives the name of the doctor who will perform the operation. It also says how high the operating table should be and the doctor's glove size. For this operation, she will be working with her friend Will, another surgical technologist.

With the case paperwork comes a pan. The pan is a container of the instruments needed for the surgery. It comes on a cart with supplies for the operation. Will pushes this cart to the operating room where the surgery will be done.

Some surgical technologists work with veterinarians.

Amy scrubs in, or washes up really well, and prepares to enter a sterile environment. She puts on a surgical mask. It covers her nose and mouth. Then she washes her hands and arms thoroughly with soap and water or with a special cleanser. She puts on gloves and a gown to cover her scrubs. Then she helps prepare the operating room for the surgery.

LIFE & CAREER SKILLS

Some surgical technologists help operate on people. Others help operate on animals.

Maybe you have a dog that needs surgery. A veterinarian will perform the operation. There are surgical technologists who work with veterinarians.

Some surgical technologists work in medical and scientific laboratories. They work with mice, rats, and monkeys. Can you think of some other places you might find a surgical technologist working?

While Amy scrubs in, Will opens containers holding sterile instruments. Amy sets these tools out where the surgeon will need them. Most surgeries Amy works on

require two tables of instruments. She compares a sheet listing all the instruments in the pan with what she has put out. She counts instruments. She makes sure she has exactly what the surgeon will need.

Will goes to help others on the surgical team. A nurse and the anesthesiologist get the patient. They wheel the patient into the room on a special table. Will makes sure no one

Surgical techs help surgeons get dressed for surgery.

contaminates anything by accident. He helps move the patient from the gurney to the operating table.

Then the surgical technologists, the surgeon, the anesthesiologist, and the nurse discuss the surgery. This is called a *time out*. They review information about the patient and the operation. They also review the steps they must go through to complete the operation.

The anesthesiologist puts the patient to sleep. Then the surgical team positions the body so the surgery can be done as easily as possible. For example, if the patient needs a new kidney, it may need to go in on the patient's left side. Will and the nurse wash the patient where the surgery will occur.

The surgeon comes to the washroom and scrubs in. Amy helps gown and glove the surgeon so the doctor doesn't dirty her hands. Amy then helps the surgeon drape the patient. The sterile drapes create a small, clean area for the operation.

Then surgery begins. Will makes sure supplies don't run out and keeps a record of what is used. Amy stands alongside the surgeon and passes instruments. She makes sure sponges for soaking up blood and liquids are ready. She hands over **sutures** for sewing openings closed. She uses instruments to hold or pull some body parts aside. This is so the doctor can see what she is operating on.

Once the surgery is done, Amy, Will, and the nurse do something very important. Before the surgical **incision** is closed, they count all the instruments. They count the sponges and other supplies. They make sure all of the instruments and supplies are back on the tables. Once they are done, the surgery can finish. This way, they make sure nothing has been left inside the patient.

Some surgeries require many different tools.

Then the patient's incisions are closed. Amy helps dress the incisions with bandages. The others leave. Amy stays behind and cleans up the instruments. She puts away things they didn't use. She cleans off tabletops, turns off equipment, and washes instruments. After Will takes the patient to another room to recover, he returns to help.

Amy makes sure instruments are where they belong. Information from machines such as cameras needs to get to the office where it will be studied. When Amy leaves, a cleaning crew comes in and cleans the floor and disinfects the room.

Amy takes a short break. She drinks water. She sits down and relaxes for a few minutes. She thinks about her favorite part of her job. Amy knows that when a patient gets a new pancreas, he will no longer need to give himself insulin shots to control his diabetes. When the surgeon connects a new kidney, Amy can see it starting to produce urine right away. It turns quickly from a dull grey color to a healthy pink.

After her break, Amy returns to her control station and gets her next case. She usually works about three cases a day. Each one takes two or three or even more hours. Surgical technologists work very hard.

CHAPTER THREE

BECOMING A SURGICAL TECHNOLOGIST

Surgical technologists have challenging jobs. A large part of their job is helping people. They help people

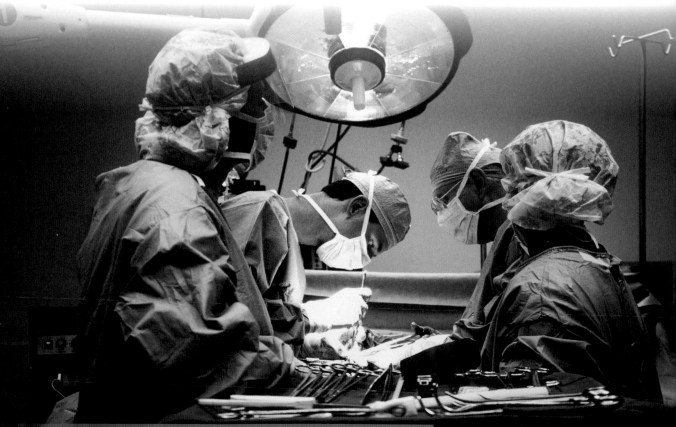

It takes a well-trained team to perform surgery.

on the surgical team. Most of all, surgical technologists help patients.

A good surgical technologist thinks fast. A good tech has a strong stomach so he can watch an operation without getting sick. A good tech keeps her cool when things go bad.

LIFE & CAREER SKILLS

Nurses once did what surgical technologists do today. But during World War I (1914–1918) and World War II (1939–1945), nurses were not allowed on battlefields. To replace them, Army medics were trained as operating room technicians, or ORTs. They learned to do what nurses did in hospitals back home.

As more people were trained specifically as ORTs, the role of nurses became separate. In 1969, the Association of Surgical Technologists was created from a nursing organization. Other organizations and more **certification** programs quickly developed. The profession of surgical technologist steadily grew into what it is today.

Operations are very complicated. Things can go wrong. Maybe the surgical team sees something wrong inside the patient that they weren't expecting. Maybe something in the patient breaks or tears. Maybe an important body part becomes hard to reach.

A surgical technologist must think ahead. He must have everything organized and be prepared for anything that can happen in surgery. Everything must be clean and sterile so the patient doesn't get an infection during surgery. He must stay one step ahead of the doctor so the surgery will go quickly.

To become a surgical technologist, you'll need to start by taking classes at a community college or technical school.

Being organized and thinking quickly are important. So is the proper training. Surgical technologists must be good at basic math and science. They must also be able to write and speak clearly. Technologists must get training in a school to do the job. There are many ways to train to become a surgical technologist.

Some surgical technologists receive technical training from 9-month programs. Some get diplomas from 1-year programs. Others get degrees from 2-year programs. Surgical technologists sometimes train in the military.

Wherever a technologist trains, studies include

- anatomy and physiology (the parts and organs of the body and what they do);
- medical terminology (the language used by medical professionals to discuss bodies and illnesses);
- surgical instruments (the knives, clamps, and special tools used in operations);
- surgical procedures (the steps taken in operations);
- clinical internships (working in hospitals and surgery centers to practice the work);
- several other related fields, including physics, robotics, and **ethics**.

After finishing school, the surgical technologist is still not quite ready to get a job. The student must now get certified. Students must pass a national certification exam to become a certified surgical technologist, or CST.

Even after a CST finds a job, learning is not over. Surgical technology and procedures are always changing and getting better. CSTs attend seminars and workshops to keep learning. They have to stay up to date on what is new or changing in their job.

This means that certified surgical technologists really know what they are doing. When a CST is on the job, patients can be sure they are receiving the best care possible.

LIFE & CAREER SKILLS

Medicine is a constantly changing field. New procedures and technology are always being invented. A surgery that is performed one way today might be done a different way 5 years from now. How can surgical technologists keep up with new developments?

Surgical technologists often take classes, read articles, and take exams to improve and update their skills. The Association of Surgical Technologists (www.ast.org) offers a variety of study materials to its thousands of members. The best surgical technologists make sure they are up to date on all of the latest developments.

Surgical techs need to know about all kinds of equipment used during surgery. This machine pumps blood for a patient during heart surgery.

CHAPTER FOUR
SURGICAL TECHNOLOGISTS IN THE FUTURE

T he future looks great for surgical technologists. The U.S. government expects jobs will grow 25 percent between 2008

People who train to be surgical technologists should have little trouble finding jobs.

and 2018. This is faster than the average for all occupations. The U.S. population continues to age. Older citizens will need medical care. Surgical technologists will have to be ready to help.

LEARNING & INNOVATION SKILLS

Every year, more surgical instruments are invented or improved. Sometimes they come from surprising places. Canadian Leonard Lee once made and sold woodworking tools. In 1997, he began working with surgeon Mike Bell on a new scalpel. Scalpels are sharp knives used for cutting skin and organs. Lee and Bell's scalpel has a sheath and can pull back into the handle for safety.

Fiber optics, lasers, robotics—many technologies contribute to surgical instruments now. What skills do you think will be important in designing surgical instruments in the future? What technologies do you imagine will be useful in operations? What cool new instruments might be invented?

The average salary for surgical technologists is about $40,000 per year. Surgical technologists who specialize in certain kinds of operations might earn more. Salary may also vary depending on where a person works.

Changes in health care will also be good for surgical technologists. More clinics and surgical centers will open outside of hospitals. There will be more places for surgical technologists to work.

Surgical techs will be needed to staff clinics and surgical centers.

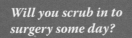

Will you scrub in to surgery some day?

Advances in medical technology will also help. More equipment will need attention from technologists. Laser technology continues to develop. Fiber optics and remote control allow more complex surgical work.

Some transplant surgeries use robotic operating machines. The surgical technologist carefully loads the robot with instruments and supplies. The surgeon puts his hands into special gloves. The gloves are attached to the robot with cables. The doctor moves his fingers, the robot moves its tools.

These operating machines allow for smaller incisions. Smaller and more precise cuts heal faster. Patients get better more quickly. These kinds of robots will probably become even more common in operating rooms. And who will care for these machines? Who will keep them loaded with supplies and instruments? Who will clean them up after an operation?

Surgical technologists, that's who. In the future, there will still be operations. People will still need anesthesiologists and nurses and surgeons. They will still need organized, hardworking surgical technologists.

SOME WELL-KNOWN SURGICAL TECHNOLOGISTS

Abū al-Qāsim Khalaf ibn al-Abbas al-Zahrawi (936–1013), also known as Albucasis, was a Muslim surgeon, scientist, and physician. He wrote medical books that Islamic and European surgeons based their work upon. Abū al-Qāsim's most famous book, sometimes called *Kitab al-Tasrif*, or Book of Methods, is 30 volumes long! It covers all available knowledge on medicine and surgery, including descriptions of more than 200 surgical instruments. Some of Abū al-Qāsim's procedures are still used today.

Josiah Rampley (?) is probably the most famous surgical technologist in England. He started at London Hospital in 1871. He was promoted to surgical beadle in 1893. He worked closely with his friend Sir Frederick Treves. Treves was a surgeon at London Hospital and a historian. Rampley assisted with surgery. He managed the operating room. He took care of the surgical instruments. He worked on almost 40,000 operations. The Rampley sponge holder is still used in surgery.

Vivien Thomas (1910–1985) worked as a surgical technologist with famed surgeon Dr. Alfred Blalock. Thomas was the grandson of a slave. Thomas and Blalock discovered causes of serious problems that occur during surgery. They were pioneers in heart surgery. Thomas created new surgical procedures and instruments. He trained hundreds of surgeons.

GLOSSARY

anesthesiologist (an-uh-stee-zee-AHL-uh-jist) a person who studies and uses medicine that numbs pain or helps a patient sleep

appendix (uh-PEN-diks) a small organ attached to the large intestine

case (KAYSS) a job, task, or situation

certification (sur-tif-uh-KAY-shuhn) official approval to do something

contagious (kuhn-TAY-juhss) capable of being spread from one thing or person to another

donor (DOH-nur) a person or thing that gives something

ethics (ETH-ikss) positive behavior and decision making, especially in difficult situations

incision (in-SIZH-uhn) a cut

instruments (IN-struh-muhntss) tools or devices for doing a task

sterile (STER-uhl) free of bacteria or other microorganisms that can cause disease

surgery (SUR-jur-ee) medical procedure that involves repairing a body part or removing disease

sutures (SOO-churz) material used to stitch a wound

transplant center (TRANSS-plant SEN-tur) a place for operations that put body parts from one person into another person

FOR MORE INFORMATION

BOOKS

Alter, Judy. *Surgery*. Ann Arbor, MI: Cherry Lake Publishing, 2009.

Wyckoff, Edwin Brit. *Heart Man: Vivien Thomas, African-American Heart Surgery Pioneer*. Berkeley Heights, NJ: Enslow Elementary, 2008.

WEB SITES

Hasbro Children's Hospital—Virtual Surgery: Ask the Kids
www.lifespan.org/hch/services/surgery/firstperson/
See what other kids have to say about surgeries they have experienced.

Inventionatplay.org—Akhil Madhani: Surgical Robot Inventor
inventionatplay.org/inventors_mad.html
Learn all about the work of surgical robot inventor Akhil Madhani.

KidsHealth—What Happens in the Operating Room?
kidshealth.org/kid/feel_better/places/or.html
Read descriptions and watch a video about what happens before, during, and after surgery.

INDEX

ABOUT THE AUTHOR

Matt Mullins lives in Wisconsin with his son and writes about a variety of topics for academics, consultants, designers, engineers, and scientists. Formerly a journalist, Matt has written a dozen children's books, and he loves cooking and baking, film, reading, wine, dinner with friends and family, and hanging out with his son.